Great Expectations

POISED at the brink of spring, the year holds its breath, waiting for lengthening days to awaken the world from its winter rest.

Heightened hopes get us through the last few chilly days as we sense that—despite late-season snows and lingering chills—a few daffodils dare to make an appearance, the sap is stirring, and animals are emerging from winter slumbers. Obviously, the glorious renewal of spring is just around the corner.

Turn the page, and you'll see the beginning of a new day in Wyoming, as the sun takes its first peek over the Grand Tetons and reflects on the Snake River.

3

Welcome to *A Year in the Country*

EVERYONE looks forward to a favorite season in the country. Perhaps yours is spring, when nature rejoices in a revelation of rebirth...or fall, a perfect time for quiet walks on leaf-strewn country paths.

Whether you long for summer's sunshine or a stark winter landscape, you can experience those scenic sensations without leaving your chair. For a rural retreat in any season, simply sit down with *A Year in the Country*.

This coffee-table companion captures the special moments of each season in photos so vivid you'll feel you can "step into them"! Turn the pages, take in the scenery and you'll see what we mean.

For this third edition, we've selected a choice blend of breathtaking photographs, eloquent poetry and lighthearted stories—all from the previous

Publisher: Roy Reiman
Editor: Linda Piepenbrink
Publications Editor: Bob Ottum
Art Director: Jim Sibilski
Production: Sally Manich
           Ellen Baltes

© 1990 by Reiman Publications, Inc.
5400 S. 60th St., Greendale, WI 53129

Printed in U.S.A.
International Standard Book Number: 0-89821-092-5
Library of Congress Catalog Card Number: 90-62426

year's issues of *Country* magazine, with a few new ones thrown in.

You'll find looking through these pages a bit like sharing a leisurely stroll through the countryside with an old friend...so why wait? Relax and get away to *A Year in the Country*.

6

A Year in the
COUNTRY

74511

Rural America, by Nature, Is Wonder-full!

YOU DON'T have to spend a lot of money to see and appreciate the beauty of our country...you just have to raise your level of awareness and take the time to focus on the beauty about.

As evidence, our photographers have captured a wide range of our country's *natural wonders* on these pages, ranging from the minuscule to the monumental: From the flutter of a butterfly alighting on a zinnia to the flash of lightning against a foreboding blue sky...from the glisten of dew on a gravity-defying spider web to the bow-legged beauty of a butte.

Some of these sights are momentary; others—carved by water and wind—have endured and will endure for eons. Hopefully, viewing these natural wonders will alert you to others you may be missing...so that you can appreciate just how "wonder-full" Nature really is.

VELVETY swallowtail butterfly, bedecked in multihued splendor, contrasts its color with the bold blossom of a zinnia, creating the kind of natural wonder you have to catch quickly!

William J. Weber

8

HURLING jagged bolts at the foothills outside Tucson, Arizona, immense purple thunderheads weave a crackling electrical fretwork between the sky and the unsuspecting earth.

MOONRISE is framed by the ''cowboy legs'' of Delicate Arch, one of 200 vaulted arches formed by generations of wind and water in Utah's Arches National Park.

DEW-BESPANGLED latticework of a spider web turns morning light into a rhinestone-studded embellishment that's suspended from a dock on an Iowa lake.

IMPOSING BULK of Mt. Hood looms over Lost Lake in northwestern Oregon, its nearly symmetrical grandeur cloaked gallantly in a pristine-fresh layer of new-fallen snow.

9

Robert Cushman Hayes

MIGRATING GEESE, driven by amazing inborn instinct, wing their way on seasonal journey.

David Muench

FOUNTAINS OF STEAM blast into the Wyoming sky as geyser erupts at one of Yellowstone National Park's many spectacles, including 200 geysers, waterfalls and hot springs.

ANCIENT GIANTS tower over young visitor to California's Sequoia National Park. Among the oldest of living things, these trees still thrive in more than 70 groves in Sierra Nevada.

GROWING FROM SPORES so tiny they can only be seen through a microscope, mushrooms—such as these beautiful but deadly Fly Amanitas—spring up from forest floor.

CAUGHT IN MID-HOVER near petunia in its perpetual quest for food, the metallic-green wings of this ruby-throated hummingbird hum along at an amazing 70 beats per second!

Donna Meier

S. Nielsen

Brad Herndon

11

INIMITABLE BLUE of three robin eggs glows from their cradle in a carefully woven nest.

SUNRISE lights the dunes as moon sets in Death Valley. This desert depression in western Nevada was formed by faults in earth's crust.

PEERING from the shelter of a hollow tree, screech owl is camouflaged by gray feathers which form distinctive facial disk and ear tufts.

FROTH OF WATER spills over 308-ft. Lower Falls, then hurdles and gurgles on its journey down the Yellowstone River, as seen here from "Artist Point". Named for its tableaus of yellow rock walls, this canyon is 20 miles long and up to 2,000 feet deep.

SIPPING NECTAR from a flower, a pollen-dusted honeybee gathers its raw material.

CATCHING THE LIGHT along its multi-hued walls, the snow-dusted Grand Canyon is awe-inspiring. One of the world's greatest natural wonders, the canyon was forged by millions of years of erosion by the Colorado River.

READY? Turn the page and you'll be greeted by curiously shaped limestone formations, carved by rain, wind in Utah's Bryce Canyon.

I Get a 'Buzz' About Spring

By Mary Squire
Huntington, New York

WINTER has grown old, ill-tempered and sullen. Dingy, pock-marked heaps of snow lie in the woods like permanent fixtures. Only the rivulets rushing over blackened leaves give me hope that the snow cover will eventually disappear.

Weary of winter's bleakness, I search for signs of spring. Older now, a veteran of many false hopes, I won't be easily fooled —I know winter can still lash its tail and produce one last blizzard.

But I want some sign to show me winter is really dying. I want to be reassured that spring is coming. I want a *promise*.

The shallow pond behind the house reflects the steel-gray sky and looks anything but ornamental. I hunt in vain for returning wood ducks...but the only inhabitants are the year-round mallards sleeping on the bank.

At the edge of the marsh, the crows guard the last of the wild rose hips and bittersweet berries from an occasional cocky chickadee or shrill blue jay. They also search for fresh green shoots in the reeds. If the crows can't find them, I certainly won't!

Still looking for my reassurance, I follow the advice of the Bible—and Rodgers and Hammerstein—and lift my eyes to the wooded hills on the far side of the marsh.

Do I see a hint of greenish-pink there that would herald buds? Do the willows look a bit more feathery? I can't really convince myself.

As I squish across the muddy field, I do notice fresh little tufts of onion grass. But I'm not sure it doesn't grow just as happily under the snow all winter anyway.

It's some comfort that the sun—when it's shining—is doing so for a little longer each day. But not today. The sun never broke through the gray overcast. No sign of spring there.

Has the skunk cabbage poked through the swampy ground at the head of the pond? It's too far away to see and too wet to get closer.

As I stand beside the low stone wall in the damp gloom, ready to give up my search, I'm suddenly dive-bombed by a cloud of gnats. I snort and brush them away.

And then I smile. "Gnats? GNATS!" Those tiny buzzing insects are the sign I was seeking...true, not the most poetic harbingers of spring—but harbingers nonetheless.

"Bless you," I whisper, not feeling too silly talking to insects. "Go forth and multiply. Where there are gnats, there will soon be swallows. And where there are swallows, there's *spring!*"

The cycle has begun again. I found my sign that all is right with the world. As it always has, spring will come. And I'm buzzing with anticipation!

When Rain Speaks

The voices of rain speak
In so many tongues—
The clipped, short accent
Of water pounding windows...
Gentle female tones
As infinity falls through the trees
Moistening soft grass...
Harsh, guttural sounds
Of splashing off the roof...
Staccato notes striking cloth
On a sheltering umbrella.
So many sounds,
So many voices,
All there to be heard
When rain speaks—
And someone takes time
To listen.

—Beryl Frank, Pikesville, Maryland

Fresh as a Daisy!

*A blossoming border of daisies and wildflowers
adorns the deep blue waters of Swiftcurrent
Lake, one of the smallest but loveliest lakes in
northern Montana's Glacier National Park. The
picturesque park, parted by the Continental
Divide, was named for the more than 50
mountain glaciers found there.
Rising in the distance against a
cloudless sky, the jagged slopes of
Mt. Wilbur, Swiftcurrent Mt. and Grinnell
Point are slow to shed the snows of winter.*

I Remember My First
'Redbud Spring'

By Judy Sizemore of McKee, Kentucky

FOR MONTHS, it seems, the view from my kitchen window here in the southern Appalachians has been the same—drab hillsides filled with bare trees reaching into gray sky...a study in monochrome.

But today that's all changed! Suddenly the sky is an electric blue, swept clean of clouds. And the hillsides are blazing with color—the redbuds are blossoming!

They're really more purple than red, these delicate flowers that so quickly fill the forest. And they herald a special, not-quite-springtime season in the mountains.

I remember the first time I saw the redbud trees in bloom, shortly after moving here as a newlywed. It was a bright April day, and the temperature was already in the upper 70s—as warm as a midsummer day would be in my native New Hampshire.

"I think I'll clean out the fireplace today and close it off for the summer," I told my husband, Dennis.

He shook his head. "I wouldn't do that just yet," he cautioned.

"Why not?" I queried. "Winter's over...it's *spring*."

Dennis, a native Kentuckian, smiled. "Winter's over, all right, but this isn't spring. This is just 'redbud spring'."

Redbud spring? I couldn't imagine what he was talking about. But he'd grown up in these mountains, so I decided to follow his advice.

Two days later, I was glad I had. Redbud *winter* struck with full force. The temperature plummeted...the sky turned steely gray...and we had the worst snowstorm of the season!

As quickly as it had come, redbud winter ended. By week's end the snow had melted and shirt-sleeve temperatures had returned. The redbuds reappeared from under their white covers, still in bloom. Now the dogwood trees joined them, opening their big, creamy-white blossoms to the sun. There was a green haze in the hills that hinted of summer. Surely now was time to close off the fireplace!

Dennis chuckled. "I'd wait," he advised. "Spring doesn't come in one big rush here like it does in most places. It's a long, drawn-out process. Tropical air comes up from the South, and Arctic air pushes down from the North. They collide right here in these mountains...and fight it out for months."

He was right. We had two more "winters" before spring finally won out. During "dogwood winter" it didn't snow, but the mercury dropped to the lower teens for a week.

I had still more to learn about Appalachian weather a week or so later. "Blackberry winter" was the *real* shocker. One day I was out savoring sunshine and listening to the bees humming contentedly in the blackberry blossoms. The next day I was huddled close to the fire while sleet banged against the windowpanes.

The following morning dawned clear and warm, as though yesterday's cold spell hadn't happened. Rhododendrons and mountain laurels unfurled their leaves and dotted the hillsides with pink and white blossoms. Meadows turned a lush green.

"*Now* you can close off the fireplace," Dennis told me. And he was right.

Spring is a glorious time of year wherever you are. But to me, there's no place on earth where the yearly drama of its coming is more colorfully enacted than here in the mountains of the southern Appalachians.

Most of the country has four seasons, but we have six between the long winter and true spring. And we count ourselves *lucky* to have each.

Larry Lefever/Grant Heilman

Take a Walk Through the Wildwood...

ONLY GOD can make a tree, the poet wrote...and judging from the richly varied arboreal beauty across America, the Master Landscaper enjoyed making them!

In the next several scenic pages, we explore the green and glorious world of trees!

So let your eyes do the walkin' and wander through wooded glens with us...savor the soft sigh of muted wind through pine boughs ...climb the gnarled branches of an old apple tree...admire the spooky veil of Spanish moss dripping the branches of a Southern cypress... or soar on a rope swing from a sturdy maple.

Our rural photographers went to great heights for these photos, especially to bring you that tree-top view above, capturing pine tips piercing a morning fog.

They wandered way back in the woods for the other photos, too, so you could take this tree tour sitting down. Turn the pages...and enjoy!

FINGERS OF SUNLIGHT reach through a mantle of fog cloaking the pine woods of Voyageur's Park in Minnesota (above). Aging cedar leaves (right) turn to rusty brown.

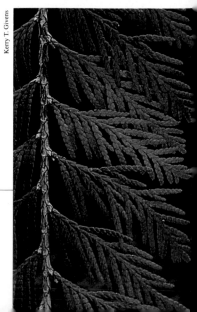

Larry Lefever/Grant Heilman

H. Armstrong Roberts

SLENDER SEEDLING has a long way to grow before it becomes a presence in the landscape. Some pines reach a height of *100 feet* and a girth of 10 feet in diameter.

KNOBBY KNEES of bald cypress protrude above the water of Greenfield Lake in North Carolina, as feathery leaves lend airy look.

CARPET OF FERNS covers the forest floor and a winding track invites wandering through this emerald-green tranquility. Can't you almost smell pungent, earthy aroma?

Laatsch-Hupp Photo

INTRICATE TRACERY of food-making factory includes water-carrying veins and tiny carbon dioxide-capturing pores.

24

Stephen Brown/The Stock Market

Nielsen

CLOUDS OF BLOSSOMS anchored to earth by tree branches hold the promise of a rain of pink and fragrant petals. Below, a scattering of daffodils waves golden heads.

CLINGING TENACIOUSLY to the steep slope, mountain hemlocks dig in their roots as they tilt in formation alongside a rock slide in the Mt. Hood Wilderness of Oregon.

TREETOP EYRIE is home to this nesting pair of bald eagles, who'll use the same nest in this Eastern pine year after year, building it up by adding sticks and leaves.

MOONRISE is framed by bizarre branches of a Joshua Tree in the high desert of California. This exotic-looking yucca is one of the few trees that can grow in the desert.

Steve Terrill

WHITE PUFFS of blossom adorn a pear orchard in Hood River Valley of Oregon, one of nation's most productive fruit-growing regions. Mt. Adams is visible in background.

VERDANT VIEW greets drivers on the Columbia River Scenic Highway (above far left), a sightly 24-mile route along waterfall-draped cliffs and forests of moss-bedecked trees. After spring rain (above left) drops of water cling to red oak leaves and acorns.

ZIG-ZAGGED SAPLINGS are stacked in a fence meandering through grasslands of the San Juan Mountains. of Colorado. Evergreens and birches add contrasting colors.

EAGER YOUNG lunge out in anticipation of their meal as pileated woodpecker—its strong claws clinging to the bark and sturdy tail bracing it upright—brings home breakfast.

Steve Terrill

Vinyard Brothers

W. Metzen/H. Armstrong Roberts

WIDESPREAD BRANCHES of an ancient oak have an eye-pleasing asymmetry in this pastoral meadow.

TAKE A DEEP BREATH, and turn the page for inviting sight of aspen saplings edging flower-filled prairie.

27

Life Is a Song in...
Rural Bluebird Haven

By Rebecca Nunn of Loose Creek, Missouri

❖

Doris Gehrig Barker

❖

IT TOOK years, but I finally did it. I've found "Oz".

I know it's Oz because of the bluebirds. (Remember when Judy Garland sang, "Somewhere over the rainbow, bluebirds fly..."?) That "somewhere" is here in rural Missouri.

For as long as I can remember, I've wanted to live in the country surrounded by bluebirds. Not a few bluebirds, mind you—dozens upon dozens of them, filling the air with their liquid song.

When my husband, Bill, and I used to live in Jefferson City, at the edge of town, it was always quite a challenge to entice just one pair of bluebirds into the special nesting box that I'd built.

When at last we located our country place, I was almost reluctant to leave my pair of "town bluebirds" behind. Without me, who would chase away sparrows and aggressive house wrens, or empty out the nest after the fledglings left?

But soon things were happening at our new place that kept me from looking back. I put a bluebird box at the end of the clothesline pole and—even though it was past the usual March nesting season—a bluebird couple quickly came to investigate!

He was a bold, brilliant blue; she was a shy gray. He did a jig on the box like a square dancer, singing nonstop; she turned her head, pretending not to be impressed.

But she was...and they moved in together. My heart sang right along with that male bluebird as he voiced his love song.

I added more boxes—and more bluebirds came to nest. In my excitement, I forgot to count the babies raised that first summer.

But the second summer, I marked the calendar methodically with the number of eggs laid...the number hatched...and the number of fledglings launched.

That summer our place—by then appropriately named the "Blue Farm"—brought 39 baby bluebirds into the world. And in the fall, I fulfilled the second part of my dream.

As the bluebird flocks gathered for the winter, my niece, Katie, and I tried to count them as they did their special aerial acrobatics around our garden. From the creek past the barn we heard a chorus of bluebird songs... they started coming...and we started counting.

All at once we were surrounded by a swirling, singing sea of bluebirds! I lost count at 97, but I'm sure there were more. I'm also sure those birds were enjoying the sight of the two of us spinning around and around, trying to tally them.

Now, another spring is about to begin, and another bluebird season will tag along with it. I've painted the old boxes (blue, of course) and added a few more new ones—one on the board fence up by the red gate, one on the tall corner post at the top of the hill, one on the fence by the chicken house and one more by the creek.

That's a lot of bluebird boxes to keep track of...a lot of families to fuss over...and a lot of old nests to remove. But living in the country surrounded by bluebirds is all the reward I need.

As the end of the song says, I now know what it's like living "beyond the rainbow"!

Song of Springtime

This morning birds were humming,
And the song I heard them sing
Was of hope and of renewal,
And the heralding of spring.

The song they sang in gladness,
Told of gray skies turned to blue,
Of the green and blowing grasses
And the flowers' brilliant hues.

As I listened to them singing,
In the branches of the trees,
I sensed a sweet, deep stirring
Of the springtime inside me.

—By Jack N. Browne, Tipton, Indiana

STILL IN THE SADDLE

SOME PEOPLE think cowboys are part of yesteryear and live on only in old Western movies.

But, as these recent photos attest, wherever there are cattle and rangelands, there are still cowboys. The smaller pictures below and at right show these modern day cowhands at work...moving herds to suit seasonal forage and water needs...working calves...rounding up stock at market time and, in between, checking miles of fences.

The romance of the Old West lives on in these rugged men. Modern technology may have made ranching more efficient, but no computer or software will ever replace a seasoned cowhand.

While the work is hard and the days are long, the cowboys pictured here admit there's a lot about the life they wouldn't want to give up...such as the independence of riding the range astride a good horse...the companionship of other cowhands who know their job...and after a hard day, the satisfaction of riding across a sunset-painted horizon to a hearty meal and the camaraderie of the bunkhouse. All this still occurs daily on the ranges of the West.

Larry Sanders

Nicholas DeVore III/Photographers Aspen

Nicholas DeVore III/Photographers Aspen

Curtis Martin

Curtis Martin

Wyatt McSpadden

Curtis Martin

Curtis Martin

Doris G. Barker

Rural Beauty in Fences to Fancy

FENCES meander through meadows, forge through fields and march in sturdy symmetry across expansive rangelands. Whether stacked saplings, split rails, tightly strung wire or neatly nailed boards, they serve as sentries that hold in or keep out livestock and wildlife.

But fences do much more. If you look beyond the function of utilitarian fencerows, you'll appreciate the way in which they accent and enhance rural scenery.

Fenceposts provide perches for some birds and homes for others.

Fencerows are secure hiding places for the flora and fauna that are so much a part of the country landscape. And even when fences crumble into an oversized game of pickup sticks, the gentle growth of wildflowers turns the tumbled rails into a scene worth savoring.

The simple beauty of these rugged barriers didn't escape our photographers, though, who captured a wide range of fences to fancy, some in wild, secluded places. So turn the pages and join us for a walk on the wild side.

SOFT SILVER-GRAY of weathered picket fence, top left, is subtle backdrop for array of daisies dressed in yellow.

TIDY split-rail fence, above, bisects rural Ohio view, accented by newly leafed trees, green barn roof and canary-colored dandelions nestled in tender grass.

PROFUSION of wildflowers intertwines with a rail fence along Blue Ridge Parkway near Linville Falls, North Carolina.

TREE AND FENCE support each other in rural Oregon (far right). Barbed wire was strung so long ago that moss-covered oak has gradually grown around it.

Sylvia Schlender

Norman Poole

Steve Terrill

Steve Terrill

Steve Terrill

MORNING MIST—a regular event in southwestern Washington—greets these Holsteins lazily breakfasting along fence line bunk on a quiet country morning.

ILLUMINATION of morning sun lights the tidy criss-crosses of this board fence in Walworth County, Wisconsin, as it undulates across grassy rural landscape.

INGENUITY of Kansas homesteaders shows in stone fenceposts (far right). Lacking trees, they used materials at hand.

MEADOWLARK MELODY from a fence post perch fills the air as jubilant bird sings its joy along a Minnesota fencerow.

REFLECTED RAILS double the depth of split-rail fence running through a cattail-rimmed pond in Wasco County, Oregon.

BUCKETFUL of Gloriosa daisies adds bright splash of color to past-its-prime fence still doing its job.

GREENER GRASS is always on the other side of the fence, right? This foursome near Sedona, Ariz. agrees.

Dick Canby/DRK Photo

Jeff Foott/DRK Photo

Ann Trulove

NICHES FOR NUTS riddle this fencepost. Insect-hunting woodpeckers drilled holes, and squirrels used the holes to store acorns.

DAISY-STARRED MEADOW, bordered by evergreens and aspens, is intersected by a zig-zagging fence meandering through this mountainous scene near Cascade, Colorado.

TEEPEE-TYPE FENCE and picturesque scene will greet your eyes when you turn the page. Boulder Mountain towers in background of photo taken near Sun Valley, Idaho.

39

A Legacy of Hollyhocks

By Mary Ellen Pourchot of Neshkoro, Wisconsin

EARLIER this spring, just as I've done each year, I planted hollyhocks along the garden fence. I remember how the sun caressed my back that day, and how the warm earth smelled rich with promise. The seeds, smaller than confetti, were gifts from last fall's generous pods.

As I sifted them over the soil, I marveled that each speck was programmed to sprout, grow tall and bloom in a rainbow of colors. And I realized I was planting more than just seeds—I was planting a lovely legacy of generosity, memories and reassurance of renewal. Those seeds, you see, were the latest generation from seeds first given to me years ago by my mother-in-law, now age 98.

Today when I visited her, she lay dreamily against her pillow. Her bloom has faded somewhat, but her eyes still twinkled when we talked of hollyhocks.

"Do you remember the first time we met?" I asked. "Do you remember how I admired the hollyhocks against your fence?"

She smiled and nodded. "I saved you seeds that fall."

With that first envelope of seeds, my mother-in-law gave me a gift of beauty that is reborn each year. Her flowers had survived countless seasons, and though they reseeded themselves and sprang up in odd places around the garden, she collected seed each fall to assure their continuing life.

And I, surprised that they grew in spite of my "brown thumb", began to save the seeds as well, thus carrying on this lingering legacy.

Over the years, my children made ballerina dolls from the red and yellow and purple blossoms, and many friends admired my old-fashioned flowers and asked for seed. Often they, in turn, shared their seeds—multiplying many times my mother-in-law's hollyhocks.

Today as I pushed her wheelchair onto the porch where the sun could warm her back, I told her about that springtime day not long ago when I planted the newest generation of hollyhocks.

"I'll come see them when they bloom," she murmured in her usual optimistic tone. I leaned close to hear her as she spoke. Then she added, "I remember getting those seeds from *my* mother-in-law."

I held her hand and squeezed it in affirmation. The skin was soft and smooth, like a flower petal. And somehow I knew that she *would* see those hollyhocks bloom...for more summers to come. Through our shared hollyhock seeds, the miracle of life will continue.

By Any Other Name...

Sweet William, Sweet William
With lavender hues,
For my backyard garden
It's you that I choose
To cover the back fence
And garden shed wall,

Because you grow lively
And regal and tall.
And bloom in profusion,
The whole summer through—
Sweet William, Sweet William,
Your name's pretty, too!

—Hilda Sanderson, Calhoun, Louisiana

Cameras Capture Kids Being Kids

FOR INSTANT APPEAL, it's hard to beat photos of kids...and especially photos of kids with animals!

The *Country* subscribers who took the photos shown here captured the special joys of childhood in the wide open spaces...of having animals to enjoy...fish to catch...and time for reverie...and for just being a kid.

These photos also show the benefit of carrying a camera with you often—to catch those special moments of country living that happen so quickly and pass so fast.

We thank our readers for sharing these times of humor, happiness, pride and tenderness. We think you'll agree that every one of these photos is a real winner!

SHOEIN' THE DOG. Don Jones had no idea grandson Tyler Ryan was mimicking him when Grandma snapped this picture on their Loma, Colorado ranch.

REFLECTIONS. After spending long day at a neighbor's pond, 7-year-old Rossi Babington sat down for some quiet contemplation. Her aunt, Kay Kite, Montrose, Iowa, captured her musing mood.

THAT-A-WAY! When you're only 1 year old, you don't get a chance to give many directions. Cheryl Jones caught her grandson doing just that while feeding his ducks, bread in hand. Ducks seemed to heed.

FIRST FISH EVER! Four-year-old Robert Kifer of Fresno, Calif. caught it on a trip with his father. Mom Bonnie shared shot with us.

OLD YELLER gets a kiss from 4-year-old Kristy Marxer, in barn on their Montana ranch, as she hand-fed oats while mom, Susan, was unsaddling other horses (and taking the photo!).

BEST BUDDIES. Christopher Mullenax, age 3, of Horseshoe Run, West Va. and his dog, Tassy, are dreaming of summer fun just past, contends Chris' mother, Renee.

WARY EYES are on Irish the horse, as Vince Kaster, Baton Rouge, Louisiana, watches him try to join family outing. Vince's mother, Pam, snapped this shot.

ALL DRESSED UP and apparently no place to go are 3-year-old Kelly League and her dog, Biscuit, of Smyrna, Tenn. Dog dressing is a regular event, Kelly's mom says.

MARGINAL NOTE: Being a grandson makes every boy smarter.

45

Arching Its Back...

Floating down Lake Powell may be the best way
to see Rainbow Bridge, a natural rock formation
that stretches 278 feet across a canyon gorge in
southern Utah. Named for its arched shape
rather than a clash of colors, this rich, rust-
colored oddity of nature is a national monument
and a nature-lover's delight.

SUMMER'S GLORIES SATISFY

By Nelle Weddington
Memphis, Tennessee

William Weber

D. Cavagnaro

David Vinyard

Gerald Ratliff

Summer is at its zenith. Days melt like ice in a glass of tea. Katydids call; monarch butterflies spread gaudy wings and hurry from blossom to blossom. Down in our neighbor's apple orchard, bees hum and hover over mellow fruit.

These are the lazy days— days of no urgency, days to relax and revel in the glory of summer.

At the corner of our old Tennessee house, the elder bush spreads out like a bishop's umbrella, its branches bent with the weight of great, succulent purple berries.

From the porch, we watch as catbirds, blue jays, mockers, brown thrashers, cardinals and crested flycatchers dart in and out of the bush, scolding, chasing, greedily stuffing themselves with plump, juicy fruit. Now and then a timid chickadee dares to slip in for a taste, only to retreat when some larger bird complains.

Across the road, the sumac leaves are tinged with scarlet, and straggling stalks of Queen Anne's lace wear a coat of dust.

Down by the creek, hummingbirds blur their wings over beds of jewelweed, pausing to dip slender beaks into orange, bell-shaped blossoms.

I know if I wander into the woods today, there will be cardinal flowers with blooms as red as the bird itself. And, lining the roadside, I'll find ice-blue blazing star, joe-pye and tall, majestic iron weed flaunting its royal robe.

Bouquets of goldenrod flashing in the sunlight will tempt me to take them home and place them in a brownstone jar on the kitchen table. And I shall.

But for now, my reverie is broken by a ruckus in the elder bush. A determined brown thrasher has taken command, and a cardinal must move on.

He won't go hungry—the full-moon face of a sunflower growing beside our old cistern is full of ripened seeds.

The cardinal flutters over. He'll have to maneuver skillfully, or the mammoth sunflower head will be pulled down by his weight. Oops! There it goes! He circles for another try, and this time succeeds.

Evening shadows are long now. Here and there a lonely lightning bug emerges to flicker faintly, then fades away.

High in the pear tree, a mockingbird is singing. A catbird waltzes on the fence. Cigar-shaped swifts circle the chimney.

I watch and listen as long as I can…savoring another sunset on a perfect lazy, late-summer day.

Celebrate Summer!

HERE'S TO rose-bedecked June and zinnia-spiced July... to the days of making daisy chains while dallying in the midst of a meadow...and to sipping lemonade while sitting on the front porch.

Salute random wildflower fantasies along country roads and the neat orderly rows of a well-kept garden. Celebrate afternoons in the sun, and long summer evenings when fireflies compete with constellations.

Raise your iced tea glass high in a toast to summer! Enjoy...celebrate the season... summer's sensational!

Jerry Jacka

Ahh, the Lazy, Laid-Back Days of Summer

IT'S HERE, so don't waste it. Take a day...or just an hour...to get out in the countryside and enjoy the soothing of summer.

A "vacation break" doesn't have to mean a week, or even a weekend. Sometimes just part of a morning or afternoon can have a lasting therapeutic effect.

So take time...*make* time to soak up some summer in the country before it fades into fall.

Lift your face to the sun or the cool shade of a lush tree...sketch a flower, catch a fish, stare down a Holstein, doze in a hammock

...or sit on the porch and take a deep look at summer's scenery.

Really *listen,* too...to the flutter of a butterfly's wings, the trickle of a serene brook, the breeze through the trees, the buzz of a honeybee searching for nectar.

As a sneak preview of what your drive or walk through the countryside will yield, our photographers have captured the suspended animation of summer in the country.

So turn the pages, enjoy the view ...we hope these pictures inspire you to do absolutely nothing.

SPIRITED PAIR of horses enjoys the warm summer sun on their backs and riderless freedom as they lope across a grassy meadow southeast of Big Lake, in White Mountains of Arizona.

PEACEFUL COEXISTENCE is rule in this serene setting, as ducks paddle, Holsteins wade in upstate New York.

PROFUSION of zinnias occupies this young artist intent on capturing image of colorful flowers in Massachusetts.

STILL AS A STATUE, this baby cottontail rabbit tries to avoid notice, not even twitching its nose in an effort to blend into wooded refuge in Michigan.

Harry Rearwin

Greg Crisci/Photo/Nats

William Weber

51

Greg Ryan/Sally Beyer

Dick Dietrich

SWAPPING TALES on the front porch of a country store in rural Missouri, this trio discusses old times and new happenings while enjoying a soda and the passing scene

GOLDENROD FRAME surrounds the scene on Round Pond dock in Maine, as fisherman carries in oars after returning from an excursion.

GOLDEN FACE (far right) catching and reflecting rays of the summer sun, a sunflower ripens in the late season's hazy heat in Nebraska field.

CLEAR, CALM water of Missouri's Current River slides across graveled sandbars and echoes the voices of canoers heading for Owl's Bend

PROUD MAMA tends her brood as mallard hen takes a break with 2-week-old chicks near riverbank nest in Wisconsin.

WELL-BALANCED CHILDREN follow the leader, walking gingerly along split rail fence while enjoying a Vermont day.

Vernon Sigl

Gary Ladd

Tom Rosenthal/FourbyF

54

TANGLE OF GRAPEVINE (top left) drapes a tree in this late summer scene captured along the banks of the Schoharie River in Lexington, New York. Sumac in foreground has just begun to turn.

SHEEP DRIVE raises a little dust as flock moseys down lane to greener pastures near Bergen, New York.

HITTING THE HAMMOCK, Jaime and his pal, Charlie the goose, snooze in companionable contentment in the shady comfort of the expansive front porch of his grandparents' Iowa farmhouse.

MULE DEER graze on lush grass and feast on windfall apples in the sun-dappled Cass Milford Orchard in Fruita, Utah's Capitol Reef National Park.

SUCCESS SHINES in face of young fisherman grinning after catch near New Marlboro, Massachusetts.

SUMMER SNOOZE in the shade of a farm wagon is enjoyed by this pair of friends on Minnesota farm.

INTERPLAY of sunlight, shadows and wildflowers will greet your eyes when you turn the page and view Olympic Mountains of Washington state.

Gay Bumgarner

MARGINAL NOTE: Three good reasons to become a teacher—June, July and August.

Overall, Kids Love the Country!

❖

COUNTRY KIDS and bib overalls go together like cows and green pastures. These two shots offer photo evidence.

While sorting through a pile of pictures sent in by readers, we ran across these two coincidentally similar photos taken nearly 2,000 miles apart. Apparently they pose kids about the same in Texas (above) as they do in Pennsylvania (below), with the tallest fellow on the right and the little shaver on the left. You'll also notice that six of the ten young fellows have their hands in their pockets!

Nan Creel of Dallas, Tex. sent the photo above, which she titled, "The Little Engineers". All the boys are cousins, and someone apparently got a "package deal" on the red-and-white striped overalls and caps. Note the fit of the cap on the little fellow at left, and the steadying hand holding onto his britches!

When "Grandma" Joan Brechbill of Chambersburg, Pa. dropped in for a visit and discovered her four grandsons all dressed alike, she ran for her camera. She propped the boys up against a rail fence, probably because that little guy on the left could use some support!

It's always a delight to see kids showing off their rural roots, and we think these two photos, overall, do a great job of it. ☀

Summer's in Full Bloom

THE SUN'S riding high these days, adding a special brightness to the countryside.

Sun-loving flowers seem to be the most appreciative, as evidenced by these Indian paintbrush blossoms stretching bold strokes of color before a barn-board background.

Summer days cast a special light on people as well as plants. So savor the luster of a long sun-soaked day...and the special glow that lights up our lives during the shining summer months.

Baling Out...

Rising from a relatively smooth landscape on a lush green farm field, Chimney Rock points its sharp spire 500 feet into the air. Blades of bending grass and bales of harvested hay seem to pay homage to this historic site near Scottsbluff, Nebraska, in the southwestern part of the state.

Chilling Memories of the Day When...

A Prowling Panther Perked Us Up!

By Clancy Strock, Lincoln, Nebraska

WHILE channel-hopping the other night, I happened across one of those blood-soaked horror movies that teenagers adore. This one was typical:

The town druggist would, when so inclined, transform himself into a ravening monster. His forays terrorized the town, and somehow no one ever wondered why Doc Brown wasn't tending the pharmacy while the monster was afoot.

Anyhow, it caused a long-slumbering memory to surface —the one about my father and how he perked things up for an entire Illinois township during the grim days of the Great Depression. He "perked things up" all right!

It was 1934, and home was an 80-acre farm.

A sorry year, 1934. Nowadays when I watch the 10 o'clock news, it seems 1934 still claims most of the all-time high summer temperatures. And most of the drought records, too.

I still remember that suffocating summer. You'd wake up in the grey dawn to temperatures already in the 80's, and the sun would come furiously over the horizon, eager to get at its searing work. By noon the thermometer would edge past 100, and as you worked through the afternoon, you wondered if you'd make it to another sunset.

Slept Outdoors

In the evening, families would drive aimlessly around, those front side vents angled back, thankful for even a few minutes of the still-parched air that blew through the car.

Many families slept out on their lawns on those breeze-less, sweltering nights. You'd sprawl on your back, marveling at the carpet of stars, and the millions of fireflies that were like a twinkling reflection of the skies above.

From neighboring farms you could hear the clank-clank of lids on the self-feeders in hog lots, and once in a while the neighborhood dogs would talk to each other from farm to farm, reporting on their day's adventures.

But mostly it was the stillness I remember. No jet planes. No superhighway traffic. Occasionally an owl, sometimes a few crickets. Nothing more.

These also were the days when circuses played the small towns. Not a Ringling Brothers or Barnum & Bailey, but maybe a small one like Sells-Floto if you were in luck. One of them came to our town that summer. We even hung around after the final performance to watch them strike the tents and load the flatcars down at the railroad siding.

Two days later the local newspaper bannered chilling news. A farmer reported sighting a black panther slinking through one of his fields. Clearly the beast had escaped from the just-departed circus.

According to the farmer's report, the panther frightened his loyal dogs to the point where they refused to come out from under the corn crib. He also testified to panther footprints "as large as dinner plates" in his cornfield.

Hearing your parents discuss a topic like that can widen the eyes of a young boy, and I stopped sleeping in the front yard at night.

Ever alert to a major news break, the newspaper carried a more complete "Panther Report" the next day. The editor had located three more farmers who could either testify to having seen SOMETHING that must have been a panther, or that their livestock were "acting mighty spooky".

Panther-Mania was rampant. Understandably. There wasn't much else going on at the time. Truth to tell, a marauding panther was a welcome diversion!

So it came to pass that my father and my uncle were sitting on the front porch one night, pondering the panther situation. Uncle Bill was especially impressed with the footprints. He figured maybe salad-plate size would be more appropriate for any of the panthers he had ever seen, and wondered if the current reports might not be a tad exaggerated. In fact, the more Dad and Uncle Bill thought over the whole thing, the more skeptical they became.

Dad Took Action

Suddenly Dad asked Uncle Bill to join him in the basement. And a half-hour later they said they were going for a walk and would be back shortly.

They struck off into the night in a westerly direction, toward what around our parts was known as "the ridge". It wasn't any great shakes as a hill, much less a ridge, but it loomed on the skyline in table-flat northern Illinois.

After Dad and Uncle Bill disappeared into the darkness, my mother, sister and I sat on the porch listening to the soothing night noises on that windless, dead-quiet evening.

And then suddenly, off to the west from the high ground of the ridge, *WE HEARD THE PANTHER ROAR!!*

It was blood-curdling and spine-chilling. It set the farm dogs to barking for a mile in any direction. Even the crickets stopped chirping. And within a half-minute it roared again...angry, *hungry* roars that made the hair stand up on your arms!

Mom—who had a firm policy of always fearing the worst—instantly declared herself a widow. And not just your run-of-the-mill widow, either. Like many folks in the Depression, Dad had been forced to let his life insurance premiums lapse. As best as I can recall, this was one of the

Illustration by Joseph Sibilski

first things Mom mentioned. She was not just a widow, but a *penniless* one at that.

And because of the spacing between the two groups of roars, the evidence pointed to two kills—both Dad and Uncle Bill. So she had a bereaved sister to consider, too.

But before burial plans had progressed too far, Dad and Uncle Bill returned in good health and fine spirits. Yes, they had heard the panther. No, they hadn't seen it. Yes, it had been a heart-stopping noise. No, they hadn't been overly frightened. Yes, they were sorry for the anguish they had caused their loved ones sitting on the porch by being up on the ridge just when the panther had roared.

Dad insisted on being at the newspaper office the next day to get the first papers off the press. And there it was! Panther Reports filled half the first page. Hundreds of dinner-plate-sized footprints had been spotted. Two farmers reported missing calves and sheep, presumably dragged off to some lair by the fierce cat.

That night, against my mother's severe protests, Dad and Uncle Bill were off to the ridge again shortly after dark. And soon the panther was in full cry again...once from what appeared to be the north end of our farm and—a half an hour later—somewhere from the south pasture.

Police Prodded to Act

Hysteria ruled our community the next day. The mayor issued a warning that citizens should stay indoors after sunset, and children playing outside during daylight hours should be kept in open spaces away from where the panther could lurk.

The newspaper editor called for decisive action on the part of the police force (three men) and the chief of police used the occasion to repeat his plea for a bigger operating budget. Our local hardware store reported a run on ammunition of all sorts.

There were a host of sightings by now, as well as more missing livestock, chickens that had stopped laying, and dogs that refused to leave the shelter of barns and porches.

…Yes, you're right. There was no panther. The hellish racket that came from the ridge was entirely of Dad and Uncle Bill's doing.

For whatever use you care to make of this information,

here is how you make a Panther-Simulator:

First, take one large, round washtub of the type used with old wringer washers. Remember? You wrung the just-washed, soapy clothes into Tub A, sloshed the clothes around to remove the soap, then wrung the clothes from Tub A to Tub B, which usually contained a dollop of bluing. And thence to the wash basket, up the basement stairs, and out to the clothes line.

Okay, now you know the bass-drum-sized tub I'm talking about. So begin by drilling a half-inch hole dead center in the bottom of it. Then cut a length of clothesline about 6 feet long. For absolutely best results, it will help to thoroughly impregnate the clothesline with rosin. (My sister played the violin, so Dad was in luck. He simply appropriated the hunk of rosin she used on her violin bow.)

Now, insert the clothesline through the hole you just drilled. Then, when you're positioned on the ridge or in the trees behind your house, have one person hold the washtub on its side while the other draws the clothesline back and forth. This causes the entire tub to vibrate vigorously, and the result is an ear-splitting authentic black panther roar...especially if you live in a community where no one has ever heard a black panther roar.

All right, you're wondering what sort of person would delight in creating so much terror. Actually, Dad was a gentle and pleasant man; certainly not a terrorist. But like a lot of people who stumble upon a nifty hoax, he just couldn't turn loose of the "panther". Besides, keep in mind it was 1934 and there was nothing else going on.

Actually, the whole panther episode defused quickly anyway because the third night—just as Dad and Uncle Bill were ready to set out for another night of panther-roaring—a half-dozen cars came up our gravel road and turned into the farm. It turned out to be a Panther Posse...brave men ready to risk their lives for the good of the community.

At least one of these strong-hearted, bib-overalled fellows had read about tiger hunting in India and knew how it was done. All you needed was a line of beaters to flush the beast out of wherever it roamed, and drive it toward a rank of steady-handed, keen-sighted marksmen.

Naturally, Dad and Uncle Bill—fearless and public-spirited as those other brave hunters—volunteered to join up.

They were gone nearly 3 hours, but at least part of that time was devoted to a panther-strategy session in the basement of one gentleman who was justly famous for his home-brewed beer.

The newspaper carried a few more Panther Reports the next day, and the editor praised the Panther Posse for its brave and diligent work.

Then, almost as suddenly as it had appeared, the panther vanished. And we went back to sitting on the front porch at night, mostly talking about the weather.

Dad didn't know it then, but he'd not only come up with a diversion that got people's minds off the drought and Depression back there in 1934...he'd also created a memory that put a smile on the face of this ex-country kid as he channel-hopped on a recent evening 55 years later.

Gorge-ous Vista...

The Columbia River Gorge cuts through the fir-covered Cascade Range and meanders westward, forming a natural boundary between Oregon and Washington (on the left). Reigning atop Crown Point, Vista House offers visitors an unobscured view of the majestic river, burnt-orange bluffs, and rolling countryside.

Josiah Davidson

Grab the Camera, Take a Walk, It's 'Show Time'!

AHH, AUTUMN! If there was ever a time to take a walk in the country, it's on a fall day.

The investment in time is well worth it, because the aura of autumn can take your breath away.

It's the season of harvest—not just of golden grain, ruddy apples and multi-hued gourds, but of sights that need to be committed to memory...collecting fleeting images of the flamboyant violet haze hanging over harlequin-hued hills...the vermillion glow of sumac against a variegated rural tapestry.

It's time to store away feelings, too—the velvety softness of cattails, and the glossy smoothness of acorns. And it's time to pluck the sounds of the season, as you crunch crisping leaves beneath your feet, and tilt your head to better hear the farewell cries of migrating birds.

Start these sensory sensations with a walk through the colorful scenes our wandering photographers have captured on these pages...witness the ripe fall harvest in all its splendor.

DUSTING OF GOLD is scattered carelessly across this country lane at Woodstock, Vermont farm, above. Stone walls hold drifts of leaves while wooden silos store pungent silage, as they have for many years

MULE-DRAWN WAGON, heaped with freshly harvested corn, rattles along rural road in Amish part of Lancaster County, Pennsylvania. Another team works in the background

GATHERING MEMORIES, far right, a young child collects gilded handfuls of bigleaf maple leaves while on an autumn outing in the wine country of scenic Sonoma County, California

Larry Ulrich

AMBER WINDROWS dry out in the wake of swather, as barley crop is harvested near Ashton, Idaho. The Grand Teton Mountains raise their jagged peaks on distant horizon.

D. Cavagnaro/DRK Photo

Don Shenk

Steve Terrill

Robert Cushman Hayes

Ivan Massar/Photo/Nats

K.A. Wilson

AFTERNOON SUN warms harvest scene above with an amber glow, drying sentry-like shocks of oats on an Amish farm in Conewango Valley, in western New York.

PURPLE HUES shade long rows of green cabbages (top left) on farm near Sandy, Oregon, in northwest part of the state.

RUBY-RED glow of just-picked apples (far left) is neatly segmented and set off by wooden circles of bushel basket rims.

MASSED BLOOMS fill room with color and fragrance (left), as herbs and flowers hang to dry in Massachusetts craft shop.

BRINGING IN THE SHEAVES, Amish farmers bundle-up wagon on Ohio farm, right, as young rider perches on mule.

Camerique

69

Ken Dequaine

TALL CORN SHOCKS form a counterpoint to plump pumpkins in scene near Plain, Wisconsin in hilly southwestern section of state.

AUTUMN STILL LIFE features freshly harvested corn, pumpkins, potatoes, apples and gourds spilled out in a colorful cascade.

Robert Cushman Hayes

70

Fred Sieb

Norman Poole

BURSTING with obvious sweetness, ripe grapes glow in heavy, harvest-ready clusters in the Finger Lakes Region of New York state.

DRIFTING SAFFRON LEAVES seem to beckon to those still on the trees, their golden colors accenting a deep red tobacco barn in Watauga County, North Carolina.

AND WHEN you turn the page, you'll see a scenic farm near Cove Creek, North Carolina, where color-splashed mountains set off the golden corn shocks in foreground.

COME FLY WITH 'OUR' FLOCK

It was about eleven o'clock on a cold, moonless October night when the geese landed on the small pond near our house. They had no respect for the neighbors... no thought for the other tenants. They were like noisy conventioneers returning from a night on the town—talking, laughing, recounting outrageous tales of their exploits of the day gone by...

By Dennis Fowler, Otego, New York

THEY KEPT us awake till midnight. Then, finally, after a few squabbles over sleeping space, the geese tucked their heads beneath their wings and slept. One or two stayed awake, of course, alert for night predators.

Come the dawn, the geese roused, stretched, fed, then rested more. The small redwood house beside the pond meant nothing to them...they couldn't see me or my wife behind the window glass, studying their elegant grace from our live-in goose blind. They fed, rested, preened, sunbathed, slept in shifts and generally lazed about, acting every bit like tourists at the beach.

As I was taking pictures, I noticed that one member of the flock had a bright yellow collar resting on his shoulders. Against the dignified gray, black and white of his plumage, it was as jarring as a garish yellow bow tie with a tuxedo.

The collar had inch-high letters and numbers—YBP1P3 —plainly designed to be seen and read from a distance. Whether or not he knew it, that goose was obviously part of a migration study—a statistic in the making.

The flock hung around most of the day. From time to time, one goose would rise on his hindquarters, stretch his wings and beat them as though testing their strength and readiness.

Finally, at about five o'clock, on a signal invisible and inaudible to us, the geese took wing—rising into the air with a burst of energy and a flurry of spray that left our pond ruffled with waves.

Turning south and getting in formation to resume their long migration, they climbed slowly to their cruising altitude and were soon out of sight. The pond settled back to its demeanor, as though Mother Nature was carefully remaking the bed to get ready for the next transients.

That was the last we saw of the flock. But we'll be flying along on their travels (in our imaginations, at least) from now on, due to what we learned the next morning.

That collared goose stirred our interest, so we phoned the Wildlife Resources Center in Delmar, New York. We learned that thousands of geese in the Atlantic Flyway are banded to track their migrating and nesting patterns. Our sighting was exactly what researchers were hoping for.

In exchange for our report—that goose number YBP1P3 was part of a flock that had stopped at a small pond just north of the headwaters of the Susquehanna River—we were promised updates on the travels of "our" flock.

Sure enough, a few months later we received a computer printout indicating they'd spent the winter at 39 degrees, 10 minutes north latitude, 75 degrees, 30 minutes west longitude—a few miles north of Dover, Delaware, according to my atlas. My wife and I couldn't help but wonder whose sleep they disturbed on the first night there...

I don't know if we'll be lucky enough to see "our" flock again. A slight change in the winds might alter their course —perhaps push them on to Otsego Lake.

Eventually, we know, YBP1P3 will return to the flock's nesting grounds in Canada with his mate. And every fall, he'll pass over us again, repeating a pattern his ancestors established long before ours set foot on this landscape.

Perhaps someday as I'm splitting firewood I'll look up and see him flying past, without realizing it. Maybe someday *you'll* spot old YBP1P3 and smile in recognition.

If you do, say "hi" for us...and wish him bon voyage!

PRIVATE REFLECTIONS.
Lone fisherman has plenty
of privacy in scene captured
by an aerial photographer.

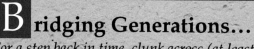

Bridging Generations…

For a step back in time, clunk across (at least in your mind) the Albany covered bridge, a red-roofed rarity that stretches over the granite-strewn Swift River near Conway, New Hampshire. Colorful leaves caress both ends of this weather-worn bridge, which is tucked away in the White Mountains.

Slow Down...and *See!*

*A*t the peak of Autumn, as we're surrounded by nature's breathtaking beauty and bounty, it's good to take time—to *make* time—to count all our blessings.

Slow down a bit...tally up the pleasures of your life—health and happiness, love and laughter, family and friends. Catalog the many joys of each day—freedom, fun, the opportunity to work, the option to play and time to pray.

Consider the many blessings of your life...and remember to say "Thanks"...every day.

Hazy Autumn Days

Crispy cold October mornings,
Misty valleys wrapped in white,
Golden sunrise over yonder,
Truly such a gorgeous sight.

Warmth comes creeping through the valley,
Vibrant color's everywhere,
Gentle breezes send leaves falling,
Indian Summer in the air.

Leaves of gold and red and yellow,
Hazy smoky-colored hills,
June has a rival in October,
Though the days grow short and still.

Hold fast the beauty and the splendor,
Mother Earth sends everywhere,
The hushed and quiet days of autumn,
Indian Summer in the air.

—JoAnn Stiefel, Kent, Illinois

COOLING OFF. "This wild woodchuck became a friend this summer," says Dawn Arndt, Ontario, Wis. "He loved ice cream!"

"WELL...HI!" "Deer constantly roam our yard," writes Robert Hicks of Cody, Wyoming. "This one came right up to our window and got acquainted with our cat!"

"I Got It on Film!"

FOR THOSE who love animals and are fascinated by what they do, every day in the country can be an adventure. Here is an amusing mix of photos sent to us by country folks. As you can see, each picture has its own little story behind it.

IN HIDING. "This photo shows a newborn calf on our ranch in the back country of northern California," writes Lanie Trites. "We have lots of mountain lions, bears and coyotes here, so mother cows are very protective and hide their babies in spots like this. The mother cows often take turns watching over each other's young."

SHOO! Phyllis Sapp of Columbia, Missouri found her wayward pet hiding in a friend's shoe on the back porch of his house. "She was so cozy there she wasn't at all happy with me when I got her out to go home," Phyllis says.

EASY RIDER. "Our little burro sat on my husband's lap all the way to Grandma's house and never moved," says Sandra Beavers of Benton Harbor, Mich. "She just watched traffic."

"WHO'S TALLER?" "Our miniature horse spends so much time with our Norwegian Elkhound, 'Oslo', that she thinks she's a dog," writes Frankie Pelking of Humboldt, Saskatchewan.

"HOW'S THIS?" Carol Spigelmyer of Fleetwood, Pa. spotted this fawn and grabbed her camera. Just before disappearing, it posed.

PEANUT POACHER. Friendly wildlife, like this chipmunk, is one reason Jim and Kay Everson like to spend time at Westcliffe, Col. cabin.

MARGINAL NOTE: The world is a book, and those who haven't traveled have read only a page.

*G*et Out the Flannel Sheets—Here Comes Winter.

NATURE'S about to give you its annual cold shoulder. Yet, while winter isn't appreciated by some, it has some redeeming features.

Winter transforms the countryside, giving drab, bare-limbed landscapes a sparkling coating that dazzles the eye.

It offers complementary contradictions—outside, the brisk air ruddies cheeks, clears senses and stirs you to action; inside, rich aromas and cozy afghans lull and lure you into catnaps.

Winter weaves a magical spell, transforming the mundane into the magnificent, and amplifies the incandescence of holiday trappings. Fluttering flakes help people catch the Christmas spirit and look toward the new year with renewed optimism.

Our photographers braved some brisk breezes to bring you this "sneak preview" of winter, allowing you to enjoy and savor its arrival without even bundling up and stepping outdoors.

HAZE OF SNOW partially obscures the sun in this wintery landscape transformation, giving frosty scene at right a bluish cast.

Ken Dequaine

Jerry Jacka

GOLDEN GLOW of the sun—transfixed in the glassy surface of a snow-bound stream in Wisconsin—is accented by finger-like stumps.

LOFTY LOOKOUT offers a scenic vantage point of the distant countryside near the Mogollon Rim in northern Arizona. This escarpment rises to 8,000 feet in some spots.

Barbara Kirk/The Stock Market

VISIONS OF SUGARPLUMS dance under the blond curls of a child hanging a dove ornament (above) and form part of seasonal still life (left) accented by the glow of holly, lamp and copper kettle.

Fred Sieb/H. Armstrong Roberts

"SNOW GEESE" seem content snuggled in hollows on New York farm—one's even snoozing!

COLORADO CLASSIC at any season, the point and counterpoint of Maroon Bells mountains and lake above are frequently photographed.

CHRISTMAS COTTAGE'S lights cast a warm holiday glow down snowy path in this peaceful and private California mountain setting (left).

BREATHTAKING VIEW in Oregon area renowned for its scenery, Latoureil Falls in Columbia River Gorge drops from green-lichened rocks.

IRRESISTIBLE GIFT of a puppy would gladden anyone's Christmas morning, especially when it's as appealing as this little Golden Lab!

Bob Clemenz

Steve Terrill

DPI

85

FROTH OF SNOW clings to evergreens and festoons rustic fence in Idaho's unspoiled Sawtooth Mountain region.

FRESHLY FALLEN flakes turn branches into lacy white ruffles along the Sandy River, at the western end of a highly scenic stretch of Oregon's Columbia River Gorge.

STOCKING-CAPPED BOY tries his best to catch falling flake on his tongue (far left) as he enjoys the winter's first heavy snowfall.

FROSTY BREATH of winter softens scene near Barnet, Vermont, as smoke hangs over snug farmstead, mist rises from woods.

SOLITARY COWBOY herds Herefords across the snow-covered, brush-bumpy rangeland on ranch near Flagstaff, Arizona.

TURN THE PAGE for a startling glimpse of where two brave campers spent the night. Apparently they didn't toss and turn!

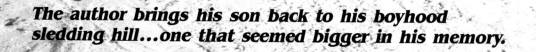

*The author brings his son back to his boyhood
sledding hill...one that seemed bigger in his memory.*

BUCKWHEAT HILL STILL BECKONS

By David McMacken

St. Louis, Michigan

THE HILL is 17 miles away in distance, but only seconds away in memory. In my mind's eye, the snowy hill is forever filled with screaming children and speeding sleds, wet snowsuits and near collisions.

Two decades have passed since I last set foot on Buckwheat Hill. But I can picture it as if it were yesterday —half a mile from the family farm, with the hill's white dome rising from the flatness of the surrounding fields, its flanks too steep to farm with a tractor. The name is a carry-over from the days when horses plowed its slopes and grain grew there.

I can still see the winter jump-off hump near the top of the hill, and the reedy pond at the bottom. I can hear the excited cries of the kids as their

sleds shot furiously down the north slope...and loaded toboggans gained speed, barreled down the hill and rocketed across the pond like juggernauts!

Now my 10-year-old son, Gavin, sits absorbed in the scenery as our car speeds along past a winter landscape of slate-grey trees and white fields.

On this Saturday morning, the mid-Michigan landscape has been surprised by a thaw. The snowy hills are already showing brown crowns, and grey ponds of saturated snow are growing in gullies. I wonder if the snow on Buckwheat Hill is melting as fast.

An excitement simmers in me. Today a promise will be fulfilled. Today Gavin and I will hike to the hill—

"my" sledding hill. For a few hours, my son will slide with me back into my boyhood. Will he be disappointed? I wonder.

The *real* purpose of this trip, of course, is to prune Mom's apple trees —not to slide on Buckwheat Hill. But by the time I've pulled into her driveway, my mind is made up. "We'll go sledding first," I tell Gavin.

Mom is enthusiastic. "Take your old toboggan!" she urges.

The toboggan. It's somewhere in the tool shed, I think. Gavin and I slog there through the melting snow. The big door grates open, and the dirt floor exudes a musty, cold earth smell. That smell brings back a host of memories, but now's not the time to pause.

We find the toboggan, waxless and dirty, and drag it across the farmyard toward Buckwheat Hill. Gavin gets his saucer sled from the car trunk on the way. We walk gingerly down the icy driveway and across the road, the toboggan scraping on the blacktop.

Few Changes Noted

The great elm tree that once stood in the fence row is now only a stump. The fences have long since vanished, posts and all. We plod along through the neighbor's hay field, watching cardinals and woodpeckers skitter through the brush.

"There she is," I say to Gavin, pointing at Buckwheat Hill.

A look of surprise flashes across my son's wind-reddened face. "Is *that* the hill?" he asks. "I thought it was bigger."

So did I.

Still, the hill looms impressively over us as we approach, slipping through the trees and brush surrounding the pond, beginning our ascent through a patch of thorny blackberry bushes. Then we are in the clear, huffing and puffing our way through the slippery snow up the face of the hill.

Does it take 5 minutes...10 minutes? I don't look toward the top as, head down, I trudge upward. In no time I'm winded...but I note with a bit of satisfaction that even Gavin is panting.

The snow covering gets thinner and harder, and finally we stagger onto the round top of Buckwheat.

Memory is victorious—the foot of the hill is hidden by the bulge of its north side—and we are now *high* above the countryside.

"Wow! This is bigger than the Ithaca hill," Gavin says, referring to an artificial sledding hill in a park near our home. I nod with satisfaction.

The view from Buckwheat has not changed at all. There below lie the memories of my boyhood—the barns and farmhouses, the snowy fields, the distant hills and woodlots.

I pull the toboggan around and set it in the familiar groove. I climb on in front, and Gavin jumps on behind. We wiggle and rock into motion... and we're on our way!

The sticky snow grabs at us. We don't exactly fly...we glide, the toboggan slithering over the humps of snow, cutting a track. Down we slide, picking up some speed, then finally thumping to an abrupt stop in the grassy hummocks between the ponds.

I roll off. Gavin grins, his cheeks redder, his blue eyes laughing. He liked it!

We climb up again, slowly, towing the toboggan. When I was a boy, it was never safe to climb straight up the hill—too many sleds flying down. But today, the shortest way is supremely safe. I stop and breathe deeply as I near the top. Gavin chugs by on his way up.

"This snow is too sticky," I tell Gavin, apologizing for the slowness of our ride compared to the wild whooshes I remember. But he doesn't seem to mind. We ride the toboggan three more times, and he takes his saucer down the toboggan track.

Tired and Hungry

Climbing old Buckwheat again and again is taking its toll, so I tell Gavin it's time to head back to Grandma's. He seems satisfied. We walk between the two ponds out to the fields and retrace our steps, stumbling along, spotting deer tracks and huge dog tracks in the melting snow.

We cross the road and come up the icy, wet driveway. Satisfied, I put the toboggan back in the tool shed. I'll be sore tomorrow, but right now I feel good. The hill *was* as large as I remembered. A person *can* go home again.

Mom has dinner ready, and we're hungry. The pruning of Mom's apple trees can wait till later. After all, I remind myself with a grin, that's supposedly why we came. But old Buckwheat and I know better.

The Day of the
Runaway Dog Sled

By Slim Randles of Albuquerque, New Mexico

YOU HAVE to hand it to the Watson boys, Tim and Frank. When they get an idea, they don't give up easily.

Their dad, Bill, was down at the Blue Bell cafe the other day having a cup, and he had to laugh when he told about the boys' latest episode. But he says it's his own fault for marrying a schoolteacher.

His wife, Frances, Bill says, is always telling the boys "What can be believed can be achieved." And that is where they got the idea of putting a dogsled team together and becoming "dog mushers".

"They watched that race on television," he explains, "that big one up in Alaska, and ever since then all they've been talking about is driving a team of dogs through the snow. I guess I should've seen it coming long before the runaway..."

The background of the "runaway" is that Tim and Frank are about 2 years apart, and they're at that awkward age between making model cars and driving them. Somehow they figured they could cover hundreds of miles legally with a team of dogs and a sled.

But finding a source of huskies was the real problem.

Farm Dogs "Drafted"

Mutt and Radar are the Watson family dogs. Their job is to move the sheep from one pasture to another when the grass gets short. As sheep dogs, there are none better around here. But as dogsled Malamutes, they fall short about 50 lbs., 10 in number and acres in desire.

That didn't discourage young Tim and Frank from giving them a try, though. For several weeks after the first good snow, Mutt and Radar were harnessed to the stone boat and coaxed by the two pre-teen Arctic explorers.

Several times, as one dog panicked and ran for safety under the porch, the stone boat would slew around wildly in the snow with the other dog yelping behind.

"After a few days of this," Bill says, smiling and shaking his head, "the hardest job the boys had was digging those dogs out from under the porch."

Frances, in the meantime, had brought books home for the pair—books on Arctic exploration, the lives of Peary and Amundsen, a history of the Iditarod Race with which they were so fascinated, and even a how-to book on dog mushing by Alaska's George Attla.

If the televised race had supplied the spark, these books fanned the flame. The boys tried to borrow dogs from neighbors without success. The only one willing to loan out his dog for the team was Old Howie Gresham.

Unfortunately, Howie's old Labrador, Mike, had majored in lassitude for too many years. He went to sleep in harness. That was a big disappointment for the boys, because they had really counted on Mike—he weighed almost as much as the stone boat, and they believed bulk should translate itself into power.

So Howie and Mike went back to the cabin along the river where they lived, and the boys went back to using their two recalcitrant sheep dogs.

"I'll give them this," Bill says. "They went at it full steam. About 2 weeks ago, they decided to toughen up for whatever dogsled trip they were planning by camping out in the snow. So Fran brought home a book on winter camping, and I helped them all I could.

"They actually went out and made beds in the yard. They only lasted out there about 15 minutes, but hey, it got pretty cold that night."

Came Up With a Plan

Tim and Frank had long conferences in their room over how to turn their dog team into a reality. Tim, being the older of the two, was thought to be the cerebral one, and at last he formed a plan the boys thought would guarantee them a stone boat ride worth remembering. But they had to wait for the "right time".

That perfect time came—you might guess—when Bill and Frances had left the farm to go into Riverview for groceries and a gab at the Blue Bell cafe.

Then, the stone boat sled was securely tied to a concrete standpipe, and Tim and Frank took about 60 feet of grass rope out of the tack room. Their earlier forays around the valley had netted them the loan of 16 horse halters, and these were fastened to the main gang line.

Then came the sheep.

Tim had argued that sheep—having thick coats—could stand the rigors of the Arctic trails and that, besides, that's the only thing they had enough of to make a proper team, seeing as all the neighbors had suddenly grown so possessive about their dogs.

There weren't any witnesses to the harnessing in horse halters of 16 adult Corriedales to that stone boat, so Bill says we'll have to accept young Frank's summation afterwards that "They didn't take to it much."

Anyway, what happened, we learned, is that about the time the two boys crawled onto the stone boat and began untying the anchor boat, Mutt and Radar decided it was safe to come out from under the porch and start some serious sheep herding.

"From what I've heard, the sheep lost the stone boat and the boys at the first fence," Bill says, "and from there, those Corriedales decided to see the world on their own. I'm still getting calls from people finding strange sheep in their pasture wearing what looks like what's left of a horse halter and dragging a piece of rope.

"I believe," Bill said as he pushed his cup away and headed for the door, "I'll have to buy those boys some Husky pups before they get any ideas about using my Holsteins."

92   *Illustration by Joseph Sibilski*

Winter Wonderland…

Tufts of freshly fallen snow grip the steep, multicolored rock wall of the Mogollon Rim, ascending almost 2,000 feet high in east-central Arizona between Flagstaff and Payson. Surrounding the Rim, which was named after an ancient Indian tribe, a prickly, frosted forest rises to meet an azure sky.

Rowing Home the Tree

A HORSE-DRAWN SLEIGH isn't the only way to transport Christmas cheer in rural America, as this photo can attest.

This gift-laden boat is being rowed across an inlet near Newport at the southern tip of Rhode Island. The area is also known as Aquidneck Island, the largest of the state's 36 islands nestled in the inlet waters of the Atlantic Ocean.

The boat is interesting, too. It's a "pea pod" boat named for its pea pod shape. Made of wood, this one is over 100 years old—but obviously not too old to help a nearby family enjoy another Christmas.

Santa Claus Is Coming... To the Country!

Gabe Palmer/The Stock Market

By Janie Pinkham
Bristol, West Virginia

TWO YEARS ago, a few weeks before Christmas, our 3-year-old son, Johnathan, came to me and asked if we lived in the country or in town. I assured him that we lived in the country.

He immediately asked if we could move to town, saying he didn't want to live in the country anymore! Rather surprised by his request, I reminded him that if we moved to town he wouldn't be able to keep his pet goat, "Andy", the baby calves, our barnful of cats, his pig or his pony or any of the other animals he loved.

When Johnathan considered that, he agreed that he didn't want to move, and went off to play with his 5-year-old sister, Amy Jo. For the next few days, I never gave the conversation another thought.

The following week was filled with Christmas preparation. The kids practiced their parts for the Sunday school program and never missed a chance to sit on Santa's lap when we went Christmas shopping. They busily helped me wrap packages and do the decorating, and sang heartily whenever *Away in the Manger* and *Jingle Bells* came on the radio. Johnathan was learning to sing, and the words stuck perfectly in his mind.

A few days before Christmas, though, I overheard Johnathan ask his dad if we lived in the country. My husband, George, very proudly assured him that we did. Johnathan again expressed his interest in moving to town.

George used the same approach I had used, naming all the animals we would have to leave behind if we moved.

A few minutes later I sensed my little guy standing behind me as I was fixing dinner. When I looked down, I saw tears in his big brown eyes and spilling down onto his cheeks. Johnathan's lower lip was pushed out and trembling.

When I asked him what was wrong, he repeated that he didn't want to live in the country. Finally I was smart enough to ask why.

In a quivering little voice, he explained, "Mom, the song says 'Santa Claus is coming to town'. It doesn't say he'll come to the country!"

Needless to say, that was the year our family started singing "Santa Claus is coming to the country!" at the top of our lungs to drown out the original version each time the song was heard.

That, too, was the year we started the custom of leaving a bale of hay in our yard near the house. As we did, we went into great detail about how much Santa appreciated the farmers who left hay for his reindeer to eat while he filled the stockings and put the gifts under the tree.

Amy Jo and Johnathan were delighted with the idea that their hay would feed flying reindeer. And when they found only a little bit of it left, stomped into the snow, on Christmas morning, they squealed with delight.

This Christmas we're again looking forward to feeding the reindeer. I'm sure that it will be a Christmas custom in our family for many years to come...and that the lyrics, "Santa Claus is coming to the *country*" will stick in our minds the rest of our lives.

MARGINAL NOTE: There's no need to worry about the size of your Christmas tree—in your children's eyes, that tree is 10 feet tall.

Spend more time in the country with our "family" of country-oriented magazines!

If you like this book, you'll love the four magazines published by the same firm—Reiman Publications. Each magazine brings you a bit of the country all year 'round.

Country is the magazine "for those who live in or long for the country." *Over 25%* of the people who have subscribed signed up for *2 years or more* after seeing just one sample copy!

They enjoy its *beautiful* photographs and fascinating features about people who love country life. They also like the fact it carries *no advertising*—just good reading.

Country offers something for every member of the family...a Country Decorating Section... Crafts and Food Sections...a Country Kids Section...essays and articles about country life...poetry..."tours" of country properties, inns and bed 'n' breakfasts...and color photos of country scenes so vibrant you'll want to cut them out and frame them!

Country Woman is the only magazine published *exclusively* for women who enjoy country living. Most of each issue is written *by readers*, as they exchange light-hearted ideas and anecdotes, country recipes, decorating ideas, crafts and nostalgic photos. And there's *no advertising*!

Each issue features a photo tour of one of the best kitchens in the country, plus elaborate food section which displays recipes in convenient "recipe card cutout" format. See why so many women call this their favorite magazine!

Country Handcrafts brings more than 20 fresh, original projects in each issue. There is *no advertising* in this magazine. Instead, it's filled cover-to-cover with

TO ORDER extra copies of this *A Year in the Country* book (at $14.98 plus $3.75 postage/handling), or to order any of the four magazines described here (at $2.98 each per sample copy or $14.98 each for 1-year subscription), call toll-free **1-800/558-1013**. Have charge card ready.

handcrafts. Each project is pictured in *full color* photos, and the FULL-SIZED pattern for every project is provided *right in the issue*, eliminating the need for time-consuming enlarging. Plus, you "meet" the designer of each craft through warm interviews.

Country Handcrafts is the magazine thousands of crafters look forward to for a variety of craft projects—cross-stitch, knit, crochet, wood-working and painting, basket-weaving, jewelry-making, applique, quilting and more!

Farm & Ranch Living isn't just for farmers! Anyone who likes the country will love "visiting" over 70 farms and ranches a year, without leaving the easy chair!

Each issue features four month-long, day-by-day diaries kept by farm and ranch families in different parts of the country, describing in detail their work, play and even their menus! There's a photo tour of a *beautiful* farm or ranch in each issue, including a "walk" through the house.

Readers reminisce about the "good old days" on the farm ...and tell about farmers' favorite cafes! Get a firsthand "feel" for farm and ranch life through the pages of *Farm & Ranch Living*!